The Prophet Muhammad ﷺ Stories for Children

Saniyasnain Khan

Goodword

Research: Maulana Zakwan Nadvi
Art editor: Mateen Ahmad
Graphic design: Mohd. Asjad Ali, Pradeepan Kundathil
Illustrated by Gurmeet

Published in 2016
© Goodword Books 2016

Goodword Books
A-21, Sector 4, Noida-201301, India
Tel. +91-8588822672, +91120-4314871
email: info@goodwordbooks.com
www.goodwordbooks.com

Printed in India

Contents

The Night Journey

The Prophet Muhammad ﷺ, was given propethood in 610 AD in Makkah. After 13 years of peaceful dawah work, the Prophet had to migrate to Madinah, which is called Hijrah, or migration. About two and a half years before the migration, the Prophet had a very unique experience. The Quran calls it *al-Isra* and in the Hadith it is called *Mi'raj*.

The incident took place after the death of the Prophet's wife, Khadija. It took place on 27 Rajab in the tenth year of the prophethood, that is by the end of 620 AD.

The purpose of *Isra*, or *Mi'raj*, was that through such experiences Allah showed His prophets many of His signs which an ordinary human being cannot experience in this life, such as, how this universe is working, what is the reality of the creation. And the reality of the Hereafter, Paradise and Hell. Allah has shown such extraordinary signs to His prophets.

The Quran says about the Prophet Ibrahim (Abraham), that "We showed Ibrahim Our kingdom of the heavens and the earth, so that he might have certainty of faith." (6:75).

In the same way the Prophet Musa (Moses) was called by Allah upon to Mount Sinai and shown some of the most amazing signs of Allah. (20:2).

The purpose of showing these extraordinary signs to the prophets was that they could have complete faith in and commitment to their *dawah* work.

The incident of *Mi'raj* took place at night. The Prophet was sleeping in the house of Umm Hani, who was the daughter of Abu Talib and the sister of Ali ibn Abi Talib. Her house was very near the Kabah.

The Prophet was not in a deep sleep. It was a condition between sleep and awakening. He saw that the Angel Jibril (Gabriel) along with some angels had come. The Angel Jibril woke him up and took him to the nearby well of Zamzam. He washed the Prophet with the water of Zamzam. Afterwards, a small animal, similar to a mule was brought, which was white in colour. It's name was al-Buraq.

The Prophet rode this animal, and al-Buraq flew at lightning speed. It brought the Prophet from Makkah to Jerusalem in the twinkling of an eye, though the distance between Makkah and Jerusalem was about 2500 km.

The Prophet prayed two *rak'ah* (units) at the spot where al-Masjid al-Aqsa stands today in Jerusalem.

Then the Prophet moved away from there and the Angel Jibril offered him two cups. One was full of milk and the other one had wine in it. The Prophet accepted the cup with the milk. To which Jibril said, "You preferred to be true to your nature. If you had taken the cup filled with wine, you would have gone against your own nature."

The Seven Heavens

Afterward the Angel Jibril took the Prophet Muhammad ﷺ along with him and flew towards the sky. When Jibril reached on the First Sky, he called out to the angel who was there on duty. "Who is it?" asked the angel. Jibril told him his name. The angel said, "Who is with you?" Jibril replied, "The Prophet Muhammad, upon whom be peace." The angel asked, "Has he been invited?" Jibril said, "Yes." Then the angel opened the door and said happily, "Welcome, the people of the sky will be pleased to hear this news."

The Prophet now entered the First Sky. He saw a man, who had various shadows on his left as well as on his right. When that man looked to his right, he would laugh and when he looked to his left he would cry.

When he saw the Prophet Muhammad ﷺ, he said, "Welcome O righteous Prophet, O righteous son."

The Prophet asked Jibril, "Who was that man?" "He was your father, Adam," replied Jibril. Jibril explained that the shadows on his left and on his right were that of his children, the entire humanity. On his right, the shadows belonged to those whose souls would enter Paradise. While on the left, the shadows belonged to those who would go to the Hell.

When he looked to his right, he laughed and became happy. While when he looked towards his left, he cried and became sad.

Afterwards, the Prophet saw two rivers. The Prophet saw another river as he walked further ahead. Jibril told the Prophet, "This is the river Kawthar, its soil is like musk."

In the same way the Prophet passed through all the skies and met with several prophets.

The Prophet Muhammad ﷺ met with the Prophets Isa (Jesus) and Yahya (John) in the Second Sky.

In the Third Sky, the Prophet Muhammad ﷺ met with the Prophet Yusuf (Joseph). In the Fourth Sky the Prophet met with the Prophet Idris. In the Fifth Sky, the Prophet met with the Prophet Harun (Aaron).

All the Prophets greeted him by saying, "Welcome, O righteous Prophet, O righteous brother."

In the Sixth Sky, the Prophet Muhammad ﷺ met with the Prophet Musa (Moses).

In the Seventh Sky, the Prophet met with the Prophet Ibrahim (Abraham), who greeted him by saying, "Welcome, O righteous Prophet, O righteous son."

The Prophet Ibrahim was sitting at *al-Bayt al-Ma'mur*, which was a house in Paradise like the Kabah. 70,000 angels entered it every day. (The Quran uses this name, *al-Bayt al-Ma'mur*, for the Kabah in Makkah, meaning, the inhabited house, which is frequented by people all the time.)

Then, the Prophet Muhammad ﷺ was shown the Paradise. Its dome was made of pearls and its soil was that of musk.

The Furthermost Tree

The Prophet walked further and reached as far as *al-Sidrat al-Muntaha* or the Furthermost Tree. This was a Lote tree, which was the last destination beyond which no creature can pass. The tree was emitting beautiful and colourful lights all around it. This was the place from where Allah's decisions descend. This was also the place from where the deeds, accounts, prayers, etc, of the people go up.

After reaching this point, the Angel Jibril took on his original form. At this moment the Prophet Muhammad ﷺ saw the splendid light, which was the Light of Allah.

At this moment, Allah revealed some important commandments to the Prophet Muhammad ﷺ.

The Quran describes the incident as follows:

"He was taught by (an angel) who is mighty in power, and endowed with wisdom; who in time manifested himself; standing poised at the highest point on the horizon, then came down close until he was two bow-lengths away or even closer and revealed to Allah's servant what he revealed. The heart (of the Prophet) did not misconstrue what he saw. Will you then dispute with him as to what he saw? And certainly he saw him descend a second time: by the lote-tree of the farthest limit, beyond which none may pass into the Garden of (Eternal) Repose, when the lote tree was covered in mystic splendour. His sight did not waver, nor was it unduly bold. He saw some of the greatest signs of his Lord." (Al-Najm, 53:5-18)

According to the Hadith, these revelations were about the following three things:

The five daily prayers or Salat.

The last portion of the surah 2: al-Baqarah.

Verses 27-39 of surah 17: al-Isra'.

These revelations were similar to what the Prophet Musa (Moses) received on Mount Sinai, known as the Ten Commandments.

An Extraordinary Experience

Afterwards the Prophet returned to the earth. He then entered Jerusalem. Here he saw that all the prophets were gathered. He saw that the Prophets Ibrahim and Musa were praying. The Prophet described the physical appearance of some of the prophets that he saw there.

For example, about the Prophet Musa (Moses), he said that he was tall, he had curly hair, and his complexion was wheatish.

About the Prophet Isa (Jesus), he said that his height was medium, his complexion was fair, his hair was straight and long. He was looking very fresh, as if he had taken a bath a short while ago.

The Prophet said that the physique of the Prophet Ibrahim (Abraham) was quite similar to his own.

It was time to pray the dawn prayer or *fajr*. The Prophet Muhammad ﷺ lead all the prophets in prayer. This was a symbolic act meaning that the chain of prophets that had been started with the Prophet Adam had now ended with the Prophet Muhammad ﷺ. No more prophets would now come after the Prophet Muhammad ﷺ.

The mission of the Prophet Muhammad ﷺ was the same as that of all the prophets. This was to bring the divine message to all people: this is called *dawah* work.

Afterwards, the Prophet woke up and found himself near the precincts of the Kabah, exactly at the spot where he had been sleeping.

This experience cannot be explained in human terms, as this was a miracle. We can only partially understand it, as man cannot understand these hidden realities which are beyond space and time.

A Glimpse of the Unseen World

The Prophet told of his extraordinary experience to the people in Makkah, but most of the people there refused to believe him. Only the Sahabah or the Companions of the Prophet believed in what the Prophet said. It became a source of conviction to them and strengthened their *iman*, or faith.

The leaders of Makkah said to the Prophet, "O Muhammad, you say that you went to Jerusalem in one night and returned the same night." "If this is true," they continued, "then tell us what Jerusalem looked like."

The Prophet became a little nervous, as he did not remember how the city of Jerusalem had looked. In his anguish, the Prophet Muhammad ﷺ prayed to Allah for help. All of a sudden the Angel Jibril appeared to him, but only the Prophet was able to see him.

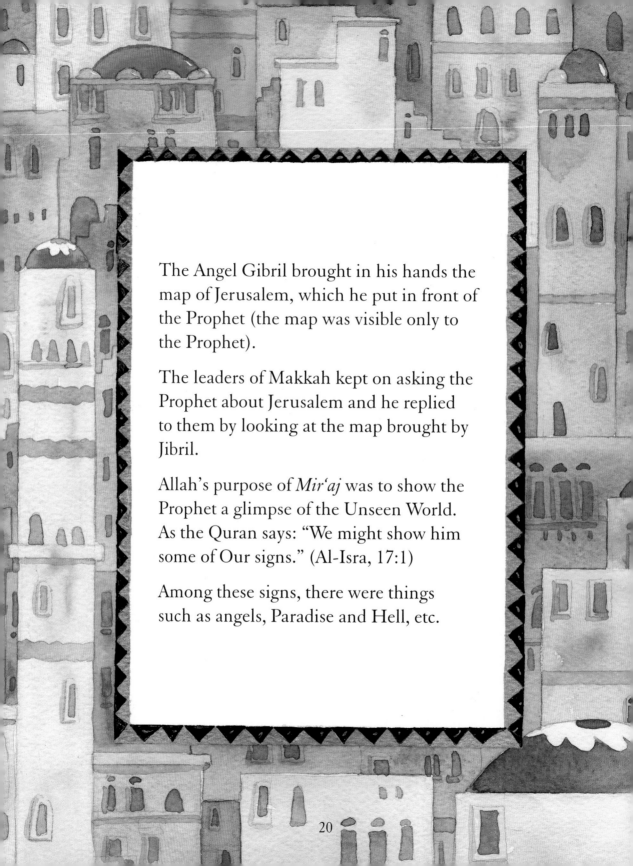

The Angel Gibril brought in his hands the map of Jerusalem, which he put in front of the Prophet (the map was visible only to the Prophet).

The leaders of Makkah kept on asking the Prophet about Jerusalem and he replied to them by looking at the map brought by Jibril.

Allah's purpose of *Mir'aj* was to show the Prophet a glimpse of the Unseen World. As the Quran says: "We might show him some of Our signs." (Al-Isra, 17:1)

Among these signs, there were things such as angels, Paradise and Hell, etc.

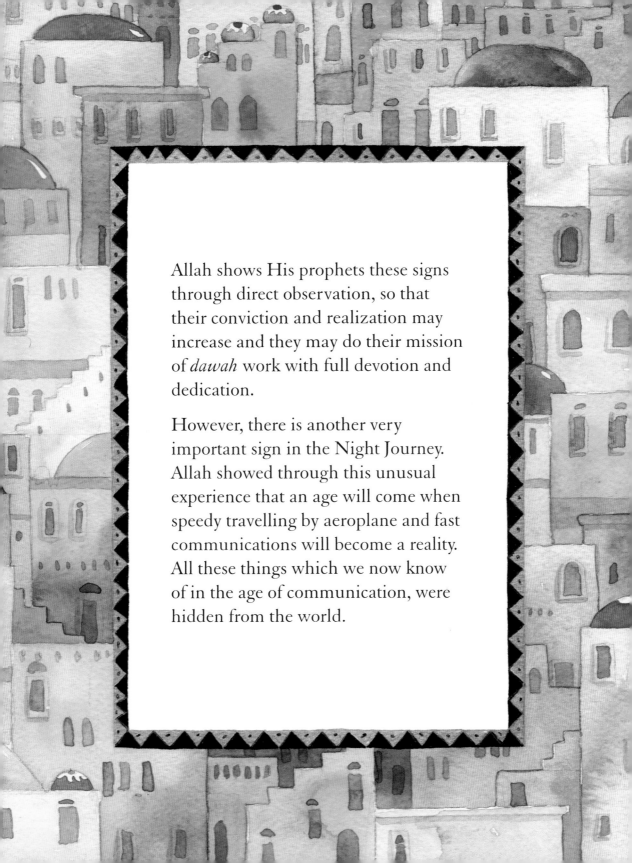

Allah shows His prophets these signs through direct observation, so that their conviction and realization may increase and they may do their mission of *dawah* work with full devotion and dedication.

However, there is another very important sign in the Night Journey. Allah showed through this unusual experience that an age will come when speedy travelling by aeroplane and fast communications will become a reality. All these things which we now know of in the age of communication, were hidden from the world.

Through this unique experience, the Prophet was indirectly told that though the situation in Makkah seemed very difficult and hard to bear, and though the people of Makkah failed to understand the message of the Prophet, a time would come when the mission of the Prophet would reach far and wide and would enter each hearth and home on the globe.

Therefore, the Prophet said that there would not be a single home or hearth left on the face of the globe where the word of Islam would not enter.

This was a prediction made by the Prophet, that in future, fast ways of communication such as the internet and travelling by aeroplane would enable believers to engage in global *dawah* work. The religion of

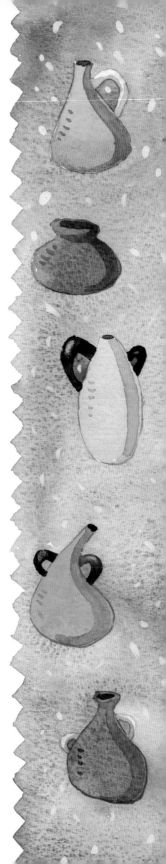

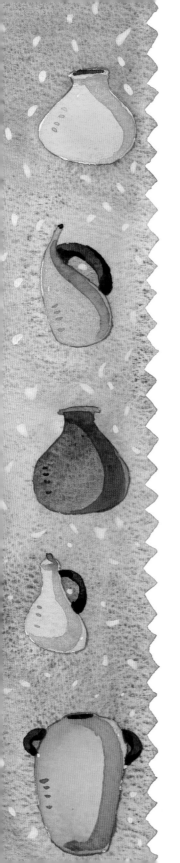

Islam, which was started in Makkah, would reach every nook and corner of the globe with the help of global communications. Due to this, not a single human being – male or female – would remain unaware of the message of the Quran.

The experience of the Night Journey and Ascension (*Isra* and *Mi'raj*) is, on the one hand, a prediction and good news for global *dawah* work and, at the same time, it points towards an immense opportunity which has already become a reality.

Now it is the duty of all the followers of the Prophet Muhammad ﷺ to use all forms of modern communications and deliver the message which the Prophet Muhammad ﷺ brought in the seventh century to everyone on the globe.

The Prophet Migrates to Madinah

The Prophet Muhammad ﷺ realized that it was impossible to do *dawah* work in Makkah. So in the thirteenth year of his prophethood, he decided to shift to Madinah. This event is known in Arabic as Hijrah, which means, the Migration.

Just before the Migration, the Quraysh tribe, which was opposing the Prophet, held a meeting at al-Dar al-Nadwah, or the Tribal Parliament. All the important leaders attended it. They said that despite their efforts

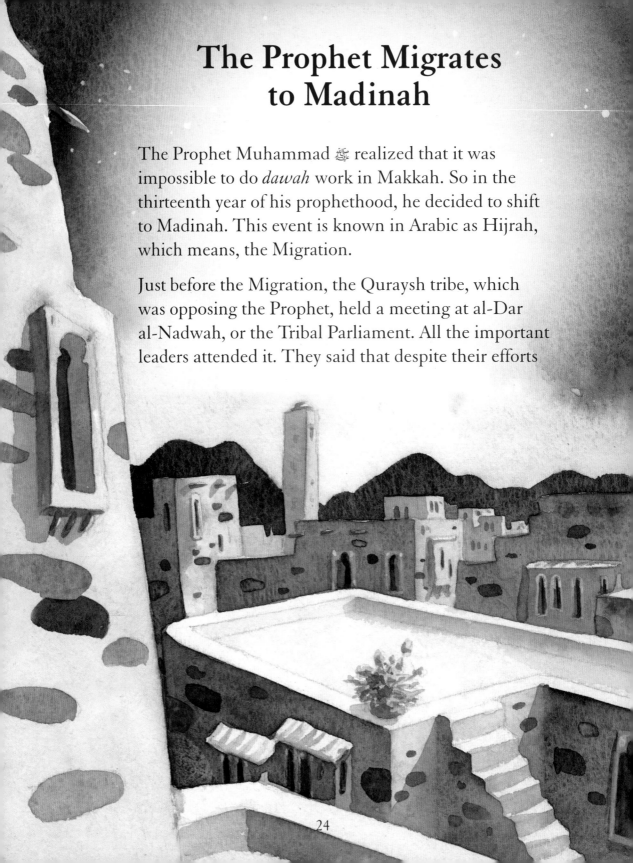

to stop the Prophet, his mission was spreading in and around Makkah. The leaders all expressed their views on the subject, and wanted to find ways to stop his mission.

One of them said, "Let's put Muhammad in chains and imprison him." Another said, "No need to do that, we should expel him from Makkah." Many others suggested how they should stop the Prophet from spreading his mission in and around Makkah. But none of these suggestions were agreed to. Finally, Abu Jahal suggested that the Prophet be assassinated. He said, "Let's select one youth from each tribe and tell them to attack Muhammad collectively."

"In this way, no one will be held responsible for the murder," he added.

The leaders of the Quraysh agreed to this cruel suggestion.

The Prophet's aunt came to know about the evil plan of the Quraysh and she rushed to the Prophet's house to inform

him about it. The Prophet immediately started planning to migrate from Makkah to Madinah.

Three days before the migration to Madinah, the Prophet left his house in the afternoon to meet Abu Bakr. After reaching his house, the Prophet knocked on the door, and when he got the permission to enter, he went inside the house.

At that time Abu Bakr was sitting on a cot. He got up and asked the Prophet to sit where he was sitting.

The Prophet said, "I need to discuss a very important issue with you, so ask everyone to leave." Abu Bakr said, "There is no one except my two daughters in the house," meaning, Aisha and Asma.

The Prophet told Abu Bakr that Allah had given him permission to migrate to Madinah. Abu Bakr said, "May I accompany you on this journey?" "Yes," replied the Prophet.

Since Abu Bakr already had an inkling about the migration, he had arranged to keep two white and very fleet-footed she-camels some days prior to the Prophet's visit.

Abu Bakr fondly fed them babool, or gum Arabic tree leaves. He offered one of these she-camels to the Prophet. But the Prophet said, "I will accept it only if you sell it to me. I will pay the price."

Abu Bakr reluctantly sold one of the she-camels to the Prophet. Her name was Qaswa.

Then Abu Bakr told his elder daughter, Asma, to prepare some food for the journey.

Asma prepared some food and dates, etc., and put everything in a sack. Then she wanted to tie up the open end of the sack. She searched for a rope, but could not find one. She had a rope tied around her robe. So she removed it and tore it in two. With one half she tied up the sack containing the food for the Prophet. The other half she tied around her waist again. For this reason, Asma is remembered as "the one of two ropes", or *zat al-nitaqain*

The Cave of Thawr

Even before the Prophet told him about the migration from Makkah to Madinah, Abu Bakr had been in contact with a person known as 'Abdullah ibn Urayqit.

'Abdullah ibn Urayqit was a guide and an expert on desert routes. So Abu Bakr hired him as a guide to assist them on the route from Makkah to Madinah, as they planned to travel by a route which was different from the usual one.

The Prophet left Abu Bakr's house and reached his home. He called 'Ali ibn Abi Talib and told him that he would leave for Madinah that very day. The Prophet had a sheet from Yemen, which had green lines on it. He gave it to 'Ali and told him to sleep on his bed at night and cover himself with this Yemeni sheet.

The people of Makkah were against the mission of the Prophet but, at the same time, they trusted him and called him *Al-Amin*, the Honest One. So, they would give him their valuables, such as jewellery, etc., for safe keeping.

Then the Prophet told 'Ali to return all the valuables which had been left with him for safe keeping to their rightful owners.

The Prophet then left for Abu Bakr's house. At night the Prophet and Abu Bakr quietly left the house through the back door.

Both of them quietly set off on foot for the Cave of Thawr, about 3 kilometers south of Makkah. This cave is on top of the Thawr Mountain, which is about 1000 meters high. One can see the Red Sea from its summit.

As they were leaving the house, Abu Bakr called Abdullah ibn Urayqit and handed over the two camels to him. He told him to bring the camels to the cave of Thawr, in three days' time.

As per their plan, the youth of the Quraysh tribe encircled the house of the Prophet with swords in their hands. They all decided to wait till the morning as they were expecting the Prophet to come out of his house for the morning prayers.

They thought that when the Prophet came out, they would all attack him with swords. It was against the Arab culture at that time to attack someone inside his house. So they waited till the break of the dawn. But, the Prophet did not come out of his house. They peeped inside the house and saw someone was sleeping on the bed. They thought the Prophet was sleeping. They waited. But, after a while, Ali ibn Abi Talib got up and came out of the house.

At that time, they came to know that the Prophet was not in his house. They detained Ali in the Sacred Mosque for a while, then they let him go.

Afterwards, they went to the house of Abu Bakr, and knocked on the door. Abu Bakr's daughter, Asma came out. They asked, "Where is Abu Bakr?" "By God, I don't where are they now," replied Asma. Abu Jahl, who was also there among the people, got angry when he heard this. He slapped Asma and went off hurling abuse at her.

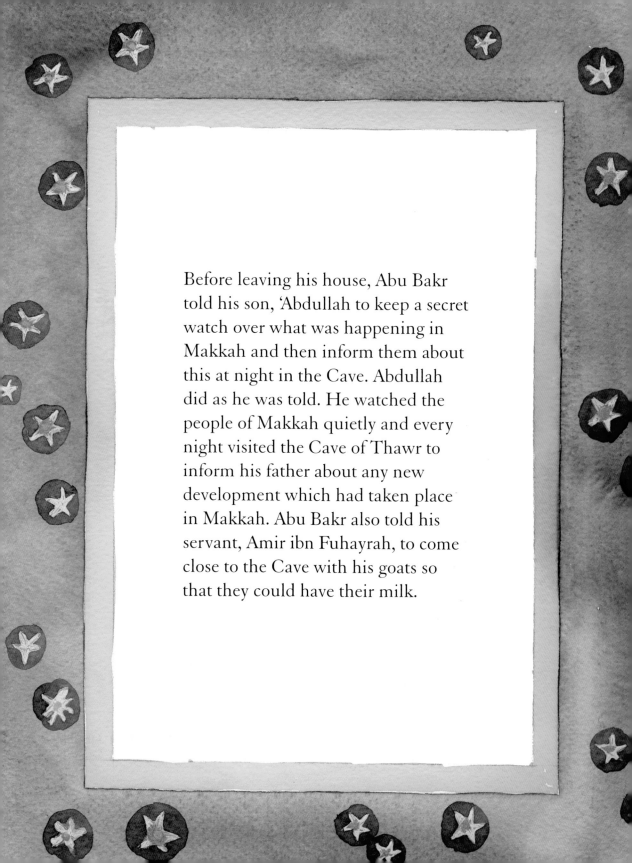

Before leaving his house, Abu Bakr told his son, 'Abdullah to keep a secret watch over what was happening in Makkah and then inform them about this at night in the Cave. Abdullah did as he was told. He watched the people of Makkah quietly and every night visited the Cave of Thawr to inform his father about any new development which had taken place in Makkah. Abu Bakr also told his servant, Amir ibn Fuhayrah, to come close to the Cave with his goats so that they could have their milk.

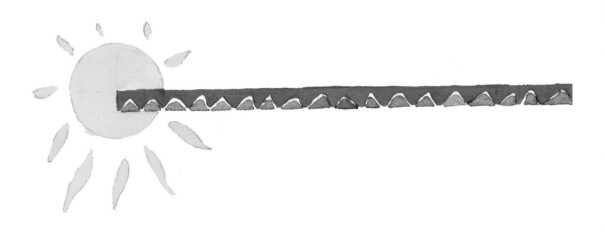

When the people of the Quraysh came to
know that both the Prophet and Abu Bakr
had already left Makkah, they became very
furious and red faced. So they immediately
sent out several search parties to catch the
Prophet and Abu Bakr, before they could
reach Madinah.

They searched for the Prophet everywhere.
Some of them even came close to the cave
in which the Prophet and Abu Bakr were
hiding. Abu Bakr heard the crunching and
rustling noises of grass and weeds as the
people approached the cave. He became very
frightened and said to the Prophet, "It seems

that they have even come this far." Seeing Abu Bakr so frightened, the Prophet replied calmly, "What do you think about the two, with whom the third is Allah?"

"Don't be sad, Allah is with us," said the Prophet, comforting him. Though the search party almost came right up to the entrance of the Cave, did not go inside and went off disappointed. The Quran records this incident in Al-Tawbah, 9:40.

Suraqah ibn Ju'shum

The Prophet Muhammad ﷺ and Abu Bakr remained in the Cave for three nights. On the fourth day, the Prophet and Abu Bakr came out of the Cave. Abdullah ibn Urayqit was already there with the two white she-camels.

Then the Prophet set out on his journey to Madinah. Abdullah ibn Urayqit mounted on his camel, and led the small caravan.
The Prophet rode on the next camel. On the third camel, Abu Bakr and his servant, Amir bin Fuhayrah were mounted. So this was a caravan of three camels and four people.

They continued travelling for the whole day. Abdullah ibn Urayqit was an expert on desert routes. He took the Prophet by an unknown route, not the one which was commonly in use. He took the Prophet along the banks of the Red Sea. Though this was a longer route, it was safe, as no one would follow the Prophet along this unknown path.

The Prophet came out of the Cave of Thawr on September 9, 622 A.D., a Thursday. On the second day, on the 10th of September, when the sun had become very hot. Abu Bakr said, "Let us rest for a while in a shaded place." Abu Bakr looked all around the desert to see if there was any shade, where they could dismount and rest as it was getting very hot. He saw a shaded place near a hillock. Abu Bakr stopped there, got down from the camel and cleaned up the area. He spread his sheet there. The Prophet then rested there.

Then Abu Bakr started to search for something to eat. There was a shepherd nearby who was grazing his goats. Abu Bakr went up to him and asked him to clean one of the goats so that it could be milked. He told the shepherd to bring a pot and asked him to clean his hands before milking the goat. The shepherd did as Abu Bark told him. Then he gave the vessel full of milk to Abu Bakr. He covered it with a piece of cloth. He added some water to it and then brought it to the Prophet Muhammad ﷺ. The Prophet got up and drank the milk.

After drinking the milk, the Prophet said, "Is it time to leave now." As the sun was not so strong now, the Prophet decided to move ahead.

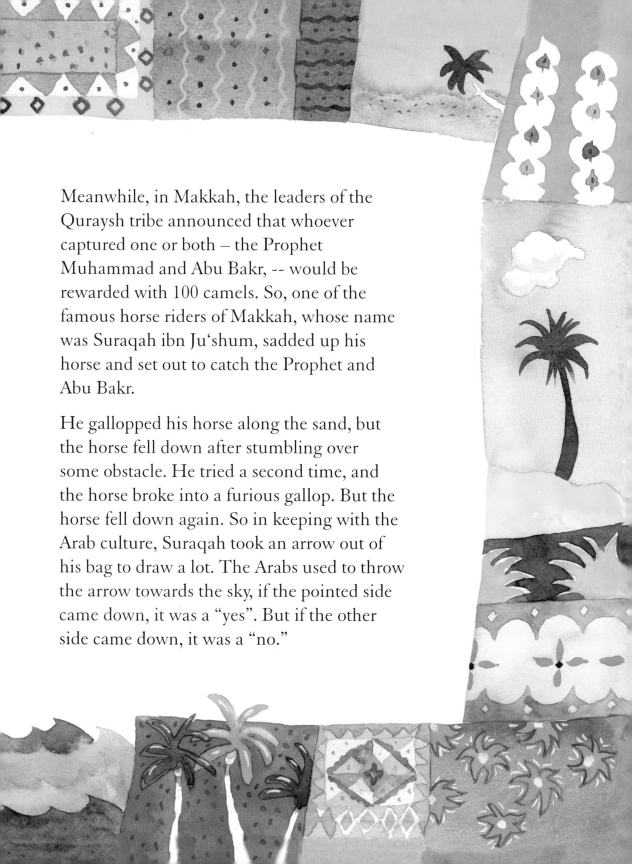

Meanwhile, in Makkah, the leaders of the Quraysh tribe announced that whoever captured one or both – the Prophet Muhammad and Abu Bakr, -- would be rewarded with 100 camels. So, one of the famous horse riders of Makkah, whose name was Suraqah ibn Ju'shum, sadded up his horse and set out to catch the Prophet and Abu Bakr.

He gallopped his horse along the sand, but the horse fell down after stumbling over some obstacle. He tried a second time, and the horse broke into a furious gallop. But the horse fell down again. So in keeping with the Arab culture, Suraqah took an arrow out of his bag to draw a lot. The Arabs used to throw the arrow towards the sky, if the pointed side came down, it was a "yes". But if the other side came down, it was a "no."

Shuraqah did the same, but the answer was a "no". He repeated this three times, and every time the answer was a "no". So he decided not to pursue the Prophet and Abu Bakr.

But he kept moving in the same directions without any bad intention. Finally, he saw the small caravan of three camels on which the Prophet and Abu Bakr were travelling. Suraqah met the Prophet and told him about the reward Quraysh had announced for capturing him and Abu Bakr. He pleaded with the Prophet to give him a written guarantee that when he conquered Makkah, he would not take revenge on him and would deal gently with him. Therefore, by order of the Prophet, Amir bin Fuhayrah gave to Suraqah a "safe passage" written on a piece of leather. After getting it, Suraqah returned to Makkah.

"A Man Who Guides Me."

On the way, the Prophet and Abu Bakr met Zubayr
bin al-'Awwam who was returning from a Syrian trip.
He presented some fine white and coloured cloth to
the Prophet and Abu Bakr.

The Prophet and Abu Bakr continued on their journey
after resting at several places.

Some of the important places, the Prophet stopped are
as follows:

Kharar
Laqaf
Hada'id
Azakhir
Aqeeq
Rabigh

The Prophet stopped at Raghib and said the *maghrib* prayers. Till today, Raghib is on the pilgrim's route from Makkah to Madinah.

On the way, a Bedoin, or a villager, saw the Prophet. He asked Abu Bakr, pointing to the Prophet, "Who is that man?" "A man who guides me," replied Abu Bakr cautiously.

In this way, the Prophet and Abu Bakr passed through many places and reached Quba on 20 September 622. Quba was a village near Madinah at that time, but now it is part of Madinah. In those days it was about 3 miles away from Madinah.

Even before the Prophet's arrival at Quba, the people of Madinah came to know that the Prophet was coming. So, the people of Madinah were eagerly waiting for him. They would come out of their houses every day in the morning climb up the nearby hillocks and trees and look out for the Prophet.

One afternoon, as the people of Madinah were waiting for the Prophet, one of the Jews saw from the top of his fort that two people coming on camels. He thought, these must be the same two people, for whom the people of Madinah are so eagerly waiting. He shouted out loudly, saying, "O people, they are here, the ones for whom you have been waiting."

The people climbed up on the fort and exclaimed joyfully, "*Allahu Akbar*," meaning God is great!

The children of Madinah sang beautiful songs:

Tala'l badru 'alayna....

There were many houses belonging to the Ansar (the Muslims of Madinah) in Quba. The most prominent family in Quba was the clan of 'Amr bin 'Awf. The leader of this clan was Kulthum bin al-Hadam.

In Quba the Prophet stayed at the house of Kulthum bin al-Hadam.

The family of Amr bin al-'Awf warmly welcomed the Prophet, and said, "*Allahu Akbar*."

When the people of Madinah came to know that the Prophet had arrived in Quba, they started arriving Quba in large numbers to meet the Prophet.

Many Companions of the Prophet, who had migrated before the Prophet from Makkah to Madinah, were staying with the family of 'Amr bin 'Awf. Some of the names of the Sahabah, or Companions, who were staying at Quba are as follows:

Abu Ubaybah

Miqdad

Safwan

Umayr bin Awf

Ali bin Abi Talib arrived in Quba three days after the Prophet had reached Quba. He also stayed with the Prophet in Quba.

The Mosque of Quba

The Prophet lived at Quba for 14 days.

Three days after arrival at Quba, the Prophet built a mosque there. It is known as the Quba Mosque. This mosque is mentioned in the Quran in the following words:

Do not set foot in it. Only a house of worship, founded from the very first day upon piety, is worthy of your setting foot therein. In it are men who love to be purified and God loves those who purify themselves. (9:108)

There was a piece of land belonging to 'Amr bin Awf, which was used to dry dates. The Prophet laid the foundation of the Quba Mosque on this land.

The Prophet and his Companions took part in the construction of the mosque for which they took stones from the nearby hills. When the Companions would see the Prophet carrying a stone in his hands, they would say, "Prophet, please do not carry it yourself, we will do it." The Prophet would say, "All right." But after some time he

would again go and carry stones in his hands. In this way this mosque was built. At this time 'Abdullah bin Rawaha, who was one of the Companions, was also a poet.

He would read out couplets to encourage the Companions:

Those are successful who are building the mosque,

They read the Quran, standing and sitting,

They stand at night worshipping their Lord.

Sometimes the Prophet also would repeat these couplets.

In this way the Prophet Muhammad ﷺ and the Companions built the Quba Mosque, which is known to be the first mosque built in Islam.

It was a simple mosque. Its walls were made of stones. Its roof was made of the dried leaves of the date palm. Its pillars were made from the trunks of the date palm trees.

After staying for 14 days in Quba the Prophet left for Madinah. On the way he offered Jum'ah prayer at the locality of Banu Salim.

When the people came to know about it, they gathered there in large numbers. People stood on both the sides of the road to greet and welcome the Prophet. On the way the houses belonging to many tribes and families of the Ansar were passed.

The leaders of the tribes would say to the Prophet, "O Prophet of God, please come to our house. Our house and our property and belongings are all yours. Please come and stay with us." The Prophet would thank them and pray for them and would move forward. When the Prophet was about to reach Madinah, the people of Madinah were so happy that the women climbed on to the top of their houses and the children sang songs:

Tala'al badru 'alayna....

In this way the Prophet moved forward. When the Prophet arrived, at the tribe of the Banu Najjar, the children were singing and beating tambourines or duff:

Nahnu jawarin min Bani Najjri

Ya habbaza Muhammadan min jaari.

We are the girls of the tribe of the Banu Najjar

What a good neighbour is Muhammad.

When the Prophet saw these little girls singing, he smiled for he liked it. The Prophet encouraged them by saying, "I love you all."

The Prophet moved forward and entered the area of the tribe of the Banu Najjar.

The Prophet's Host

Everyone in Madinah was expecting that the Prophet would stay in his house. The Prophet said that he would stay with the tribe of the Banu Najjar, as he was the uncle of his grandfather, Abdul Muttalib. Also, the wife of Abdul Muttalib was from the family of the Banu Najjar.

Abu Ayyub al-Ansari belonged to the same family, and so, the Prophet stayed at his house. The house of Abu Ayyub al-Ansari was a double storied house. Abu Ayyub asked the Prophet to stay on the upper floor of the house, but the Prophet preferred to live on the ground floor, as many people were visiting him throughout the day.

There was a big vessel which was kept on the upper floor of Abu Ayyub al-Ansari's house. It was used for storing water. One day it got broken. The roof was made of wood, so, he feared that water from the upper floor might trickle downstairs. Abu Ayyub had a big thick quilt. So he quickly threw it on the floor, so that it could soak up the spilled water.

The Prophet Muhammad ﷺ lived for about seven months in the house of Abu Ayyub al-Ansari. During this period, the Prophet built the mosque in Madinah, which is now known as al-Masjid al-Nabawi, or the Prophet's Mosque.

Before the mosque was built, the Companions would say their prayers wherever there was space – in houses, outside on the sand, on the

hillocks, or in the date palm orchids. Then the Prophet thought of building a mosque so that the Companions could pray there and it would act as a centre for learning and *dawah* planning in and around Madinah.

There was an open plot of land near the house of Abu Ayyub al-Ansari, which belonged to the family of the Banu al-Najjar. This land was mainly used for drying the dates. On one side of this land, there were some old graves as well. There were some of dates palm on the other side of the land.

The Prophet called the people of the family of the Banu Najjar and told them that he wanted to buy this piece of land. They said, "We will not take any money for it for we expect the reward from Allah." But the Prophet insisted that he would take the land only if they agreed to sell it. They said that this land belonged to two orphans, Sahl and Suhayl. They called the two brothers to meet the Prophet.

When Sahl and Suhayl came to meet the Prophet, the Prophet told them that he was willing to buy this piece of land from them. They happily offered the land to the Prophet without taking any money for it. But the Prophet insisted on paying the cost of the land. Therefore, on behalf of the Prophet, Abu Ayyub al-Ansari bought the piece of land from Sahl and Suhayl by paying them its cost.

Afterwards, the land was cleared of all the unwanted wild plants, grass, weeds and cactus, etc., which had grown up all over it, the old graves were dismantled and the ground was levelled. When the land had been cleaned and properly levelled, the construction of the mosque was started.

The Prophet's Mosque

The Prophet Muhammad ﷺ and the Sahabah (Companions) took part in the building of the mosque. The Companions would bring stones from the nearby hills, and they would recite such couplets:

Allahumma la 'aysha illal 'ayshal-akhirah

Faghfir lil ansari wal muhajarah

O Allah, the real life is the life hereafter.

O Allah, grant success to the Ansar and Muhajirs.

The Prophet would often say these words along with the Companions.

In this way, the mosque was built at Madinah. It was a simple mosque, which was made of stones and bricks. The walls were covered with leaves of the date palm. The trunks of date palm trees were used as pillars to support the roof which was made of the dried leaves of date palm trees.

The *qiblah*, or the prayer direction, which was towards Jerusalem, remained unchanged for sixteen months. The Jews used to pray in the direction of Jerusalem and the Prophet adopted the same prayer direction in the beginning. Later it was changed to Makkah in accordance with the revelation of the Quran. Therefore a *mihrab*, or niche, was made in the wall of the mosque pointing towards Makkah.

The floor of the mosque was made of sand and mud. Whenever there was rain, it would become wet and muddy.

Later, the Prophet had the entire floor of the mosque covered with small pebbles to make it easier for those who prayed there.

When the mosque was completed, the Prophet had two rooms built right next to the mosque for his wives, Aisha and Sawda.

The Prophet then decided to send someone to Makkah to bring his family to Madinah, as at that time, the Prophet's family were still staying in Makkah. So he gave two camels and 500 dirhams to Zayd ibn Haritha and his assistant, Abu Rafi', to go to Makkah and bring his family from there. Abu Bakr also wrote a letter to his son, Abdullah, to bring his mother and sisters to Madinah.

Ruqayya, one of the Prophet's daughters, was not in Makkah. She was living in Abyssinia (Ethiopia) along with her husband, 'Uthman bin Affan.

Zaynab, the Prophet's other daughter, was in Makkah, but her husband did not allow her to go to Madinah.

So, Zayd brought the Prophet's two daughters, Fatimah and Umm Kulthum, along with his wife, Sawda bint Zam'a, to Madinah.

Aishah, along with her brother, Abdullah, and her mother, Umma Ruman, also reached Madinah.

When other members of the Prophet's family arrived in Madinah, he had a few more rooms built alongside the Prophet's mosque.

These rooms were simple structures, the walls of which were made of mud and stones and the roofs were made of the dried leaves of date palm trees. The size of these rooms was about 10 feet by 15 feet. The height of the roof was about 7 feet. One could easily touch the roof with one's hands.

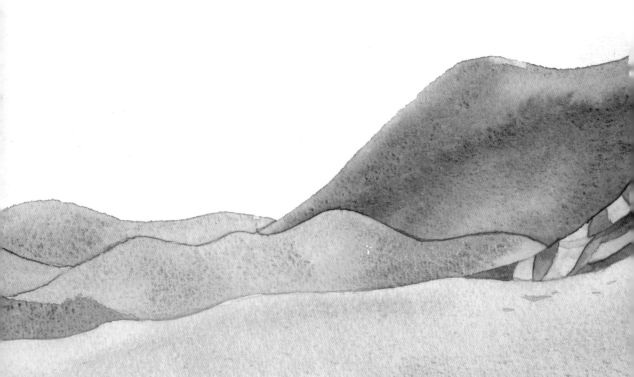

In those days there were no lamps to light up at night. Many years later, one of the Companions was surprised to learn that there had been no lamps in the Prophet's house to light up at night. He asked Aisha in wonder, "Was there were no oil in your house then?" To which Aisha replied, "We were in such difficulty that if we had had oil in our house, instead of lighting a lamp, we would have drunk it." In those days there was no petrol or kerosene oil, so edible oil, such as olive oil, was used to light the lamps. This shows in what difficult conditions the Prophet and his family lived in Madinah.

In Madinah, there were many of the Sahabah living in the neighbourhood of the Prophet, such as Sa'd bin Ubadah, Sa'd bin Ma'adh, 'Ammarah bin Hazam, Abu Ayyub al-Ansari, etc. They would send milk and food to the Prophet's family on a regular basis.

Every night Sa'd bin Ubadah would send a big wooden bowl full of curry or milk or butter or cheese to the Prophet's house.

Umm Anas, the mother of Anas, gifted an orchard of date palm trees and a camel to the Prophet, which he gifted to Umm Aiyman, who had nursed how the Prophet in his childhood. Umm Aiman was the maid of the Prophet's mother, Amina.

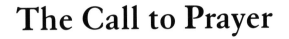

The Call to Prayer

When the Mosque was built in Madinah, which is known as the Prophet's Mosque, the Companions started to pray there. But there was no system of praying together in congregation. People used to pray on their own. For this reason there was no discipline, and the Prophet did not like this.

He thought that some people should be appointed to go and fetch people at the time of prayer. So some people were appointed for this purpose. But he later realized that this was not a practical way to do things.

Then the Prophet called the Sahabah and discussed this with them. People made different suggestions. Someone said, let's put up a long flag at the time of prayer, so that people would come to know that it was now time to go to the mosque. Some of them suggested that at the time of the prayer, a trumpet should be sounded from the mosque and, hearing this, people would get to know that it was time for prayer. But the Prophet did not like such suggestions.

Then Umar ibn al-Khattab, suggested that at the time of prayer, some one should announce loudly from the mosque that, "Prayer is about to start" – *As-salatu jami'atun*. So a person stood on a raised platform in the mosque and called out to the people, *As-salatu jami'atun*.

The Prophet later saw in a dream that someone was saying the words which we now hear in the *adhan*, or the call to prayer today. Other Sahabah, including 'Umar bin al-Khattab and 'Abdullah bin Zayd, also had similar dreams. When they all met the Prophet and told of their dreams, the Prophet thought that it was a message from Allah that we should use these words to call people to prayer.

Then the Prophet called Bilal bin Rabah and asked him to give the call for prayer (*adhan*) by calling out the following words:

Allahu Akbar, Allahu Akbar.
Allah is the Greatest, Allah is the Greatest. (twice)
Ash-hadu alla ilaha illa-llah.
I bear witness that there is none worthy of worship but Allah. (twice)
Ash-hadu anna Muhammadar-Rasulullah.
I bear witness that Muhammad is the Messenger of Allah (twice)
Hayya 'ala-s-Salah, hayya 'ala-s-Salah.
Hasten to the Prayer, hasten to the Prayer.
Hayya 'ala-l-falah, hayya 'ala-l-falah.
Hasten to real success, hasten to real success
Allahu Akbar, Allahu Akbar.
Allah is the Greatest, Allah is the Greatest.
La ilaha illa-llah
There is none worthy of worship but Allah.
In this way the *adhan* and *salat* (prayers) were properly started in the Prophet's Mosque.

The First Sermon
in Madinah

Then the Prophet Muhammad ﷺ asked people
to gather in the mosque and gave two short
sermons. These sermons the first given by the
Prophet in Madinah, are mentioned in the
books on the life of the Prophet.

The Prophet stood up and first praised and
glorified Allah and then thanked Him. Then he
addressed the people and told them to prepare
for their Hereafter (*akhirah*). He said that very
soon "for each one of you, the Day is coming

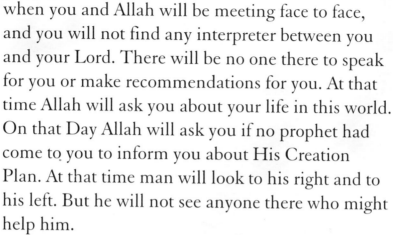

when you and Allah will be meeting face to face, and you will not find any interpreter between you and your Lord. There will be no one there to speak for you or make recommendations for you. At that time Allah will ask you about your life in this world. On that Day Allah will ask you if no prophet had come to you to inform you about His Creation Plan. At that time man will look to his right and to his left. But he will not see anyone there who might help him.

At that time there will be either Paradise forever or hell forever. So save yourself from the hell fire, even if only by doing a small good deed. By saying so, the Prophet meant that one should not think that a small good deed had no value in the eyes of Allah.

The Prophet continued his sermon. If anyone did not have anything to spend on a good cause, he should just say something good. He should call people to do good things as one good deed may be multiplied up to 700 fold.

According to the word of the Prophet, this world is the first and the last chance for a man. So whenever, he gets an opportunity to do good, he should not let it go, even if it is only be doing a small act of goodness.

Every good act whether small or big, will benefit the life of man in the Hereafter, the life which will never end.

Afterwards, the Prophet ended his sermon saying, *Wassalamu alaykum wa rahmatul'lah wa barakatuhu*, may peace and blessing be upon you all!

After some days, the Prophet Muhammad ﷺ told the people to gather in the Mosque. When a number of the people had gathered, the Prophet got up and stood on the *minbar*, a small raised platform. He began saying, All praise and all thanks belongs to Allah, I seek help from Him alone. I seek Allah's help and I seek Allah's help from evil deeds. If Allah guides a person to the right path, no one can make him go astray. But no one can guide anyone who is allowed to go

astray by Allah. I bear witness that there is no deity worth worshipping other than Him. He is the only One who should be worshipped. No one is His partner. The best words are the words of Allah's Book, that is, the Quran. The one who is given a knowledge of the Quran will be successful. Out of everything, Allah has made the Quran the best, You love the Quran—the Book of God, you love the one who loves Allah.

Afterwards the Prophet said that you should love Allah with all your heart and soul. "Do not be lazy in doing so. Fill your hearts with Allah's love and remembrance. The greatest thing of this world is remembrance of Allah, and to follow the path which is ordered by Allah. So worship none other than Allah, and do not worship anyone other than Allah. You should fear God with full justice. You should always say what is good and true. You should always fulfill your promise, as Allah will be angry with anyone who breaks His promise." The Prophet finished his sermon by saying "*Was-salamu alaykum wa rahmatullah.*"

The Platform of al-Suffa

When the Prophet Muhammad ﷺ started the
prayers at the Prophet's Mosque in Madinah,
he made Jerusalem the *qiblah*, or prayer direction.
Therefore the Prophet and the Sahabah prayed
towards Jerusalem for 16 months. Afterwards,
Allah commanded the Prophet to change his *qiblah*
towards Makkah.

Earlier when they used to pray towards Jerusalem,
there was a niche (*mihrab*) in one of the walls of
the mosque pointing towards Jerusalem.

But when the *qiblah* was changed to Makkah,
those saying their prayers had to face in the
opposite direction. At that time, the area where the
previous *mihrab* had been situated, was covered by
date palm leaves by the Prophet. Then that area,
which was at the back of the mosque, was called
al-Suffah. People would come and stay there.
Those Sahabah who migrated from Makkah,

would generally first stay at this place, then move to some other place. So it served as an inn for these migrating from Makkah to Madinah. About 400 Sahabah stayed there at different times.

The people who stayed at Suffah would talk to ea chother about the Quran. They would read the Quran, learn from each other, pray and pass on knowledge to others. They dedicated their lives to the cause of Islam.

The most notable among the People of Suffah was Abu Hurayrah, whose contribution to the Hadith was very great. He would remain in the Mosque all the time and would lead a very simple life. He would be contented with whatever he got to eat. In this way, he was able to collect more than five thousand sayings of the Prophet, which is the most precious treasure of Islamic teachings.

Some of the notable Sahabah who stayed at the Suffah are as follows:

Abu Hurayrah
Abu Dharr Ghifari
Ka'b bin Malik
Salman Farsi
Khabbab bin Arat
Abdullah bin Mas'ud
Suhayb al-Rumi
Bilal bin Rabah

The Prophet would send the team of the Ashab al-Suffah to various places to do *dawah* work.

Most of these people were not married, when one of them married a woman in Madinah, he would move out from the Mosque.

Some of the people of Suffah would go to the jungle to cut the wood of trees and bring it back to Madinah to sell.

As part of the Arab culture, many people used to rear camels and goats. Ground date seed powder would be used for food for the sheep and camels. The people of Suffah would do the grinding of date seeds to make the fodder for camels and goats. In this way they would earn their living.

The Muslims of Madinah, the Ansar, would regularly send food for them. When the Prophet received some gifts, he would also send gifts to the People of Suffah.

Sometimes, one of the rich Muslims, like Sa'd bin Ubadah, would take them to his home. Sometimes as many as eighty people from the People of the Suffah would go with Sa'd bin Ubadah for a meal.

The Prophet always took great care of the People of the Suffah and would personally teach them the Quran and pass on his wisdom to them.

Because of their exceptional dedication and sacrifice, the People of the Suffah have a great place in the history of the early period of Islam.

The Ansar or the Helpers

The Prophet Muhammad ﷺ migrated from Makkah to Madinah in 622 A.D. At that time, there were two big groups, the *Ansar* and the Jews. The *Ansar* were the Muslims, who invited the Prophet to Madinah and helped the Prophet and the Muslims who migrated from Makkah.

When Yemen suffered a huge flood, known as *Sayl al-Arim* (34:16) after the Marib dam cracked, its people fled to different places. Among them were two brothers, Aws and Khazraj, who settled in Madinah (at that time known as Yathrib). Over a period of time their families grew in number and so two big tribes were founded, called the Aws and the Khazraj after the two brothers. These were the two main tribes of the Ansar.

Much before the arrival of Aws and Khazraj in Madinah, a number of Jews had migrated from Syria and Palestine and settled in Madinah in the first century B.C. They were mainly merchants. They owned most of the lands in the area. There were about twenty one tribes of Jews in Madinah. Earlier, the Ansar used to live on their own, but later, the Ansar signed an agreement with them and both Jews and the Ansar started to live together. But the agreement was broken after some time.

After some time fighting broke out between the Aws and Khazraj which was known as the Battle of Bu'ath. In this war, many of the leaders of both the groups died. As a result, the strength and power of both the groups weakened.

For this reason, they sent their delegation to the Quraysh in Makkah to enter into an agreement with them. As that was the tribal age, no tribe could survive without the support of a bigger and more powerful tribe. In this way, they became one of the allies of the Quraysh tribe.

The Jews of Madinah were the People of the Book, therefore, the Ansar were in awe of their knowledge and superiority. The Jews had set up a number of organizations which were known as *Bayt al-Midras*. In these centres they would teach the Torah and the Talmud. These were traditional places of learning. The word *madrasah* came from the word *bayt al-midras*.

The Ansar for their part were not educated, and so were impressed by the Jews.

Since the Jews of Madinah were the People of the Book, they were aware that soon the Last Prophet would be sent by God.

The Jews used to tell the Ansar that when the Last Prophet emerged, they would fight along with him to have power over them. But when the Last Prophet, the Prophet Muhammad ﷺ came, the Jews failed to recognize him and they rejected him. The Quran mentions this in *surah al-Baqrah*, 2:89.

On the other hand, the Ansar recognized the Prophet Muhammad ﷺ and they became helpers of his mission.

A Unique Brotherhood

When the Prophet Muhammad ﷺ reached Madinah, he established the historic concept of brotherhood which is known as *al-muakhat*. Madinah was a small town. When the Companions of the Prophet reached Madinah they faced a number of problems. For example, there were no houses for them to stay in, food was scarce and so on. So the Prophet Muhammad ﷺ solved these problems in a unique way. He established a brotherly relationship between the Ansar (Helpers) of Madinah and the Muhajirs (Migrants) of Makkah.

After the construction of the Prophet's Mosque, the Prophet Muhammad ﷺ called the Ansar to the house of Anas bin Malik. At that time the total number of the Mujahirs, or the Migrants, was only 45. The Prophet Muhammad ﷺ addressed the Ansar and the Muhajirs and said to the Ansar that the Muhajirs were their brothers. "For the sake of Islam they have left their homeland. Therefore, your conduct with them should be as with your own brothers." The Ansar immediately said, "We agree to what you say."

Then the Prophet Muhammad ﷺ called one person from the Ansar and another one from the Muhajir and said, "From today both of you are brothers. Now you will live together and your boarding and lodging will also be together." Some of the names of the Companions who were made brothers by the Prophet, are as follows:

Muhajirs (the Migrants) – Ansar (the Helpers)

Abu Bakr – Kharijah bin Zayd
Umar bin al-Khattab – Utbah bin Malik
Uthman bin Affan – Aws bin Thabit
Ubaydah bin al-Jarrah – Sa'd bin Mu'adh
Zubayr bin al-Awwam – Salamah bin Daqsh
Mus'ab bin Umayr – Abu Ayyub al-Ansari
Ammar bin Yasir – Huzaifah bin Yaman
Abu Dharr al-Ghifari – Munzar bin 'Amr
Salman al-Farsi – Abu Darda
Bilal bin Rabah – Abu Ruwaiha
Abu Huzaifah bin Utbah bin Rabiya – Abad bin Bishr

After the Prophet's decision to form this brotherhood between the Ansar and the Muhajirs, they started to live like real brothers. Even the Ansar started to prefer their Muhajir brothers to themselves. The Ansar took the Muhajirs to where they lived and showed them their belongings, such as their houses, orchards, lands, camels, cattle, etc., and said to them, "From today, half of all our belongings will be yours." But the Muhajirs did not want to become a burden on the Ansar. So they did not live with them forever, but tried rather to find ways to be on their own.

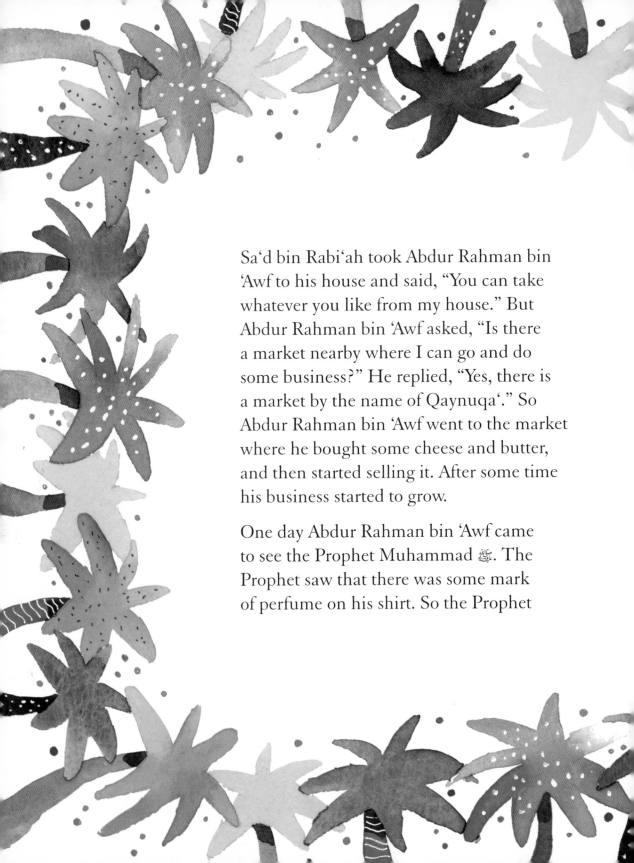

Sa'd bin Rabi'ah took Abdur Rahman bin 'Awf to his house and said, "You can take whatever you like from my house." But Abdur Rahman bin 'Awf asked, "Is there a market nearby where I can go and do some business?" He replied, "Yes, there is a market by the name of Qaynuqa'." So Abdur Rahman bin 'Awf went to the market where he bought some cheese and butter, and then started selling it. After some time his business started to grow.

One day Abdur Rahman bin 'Awf came to see the Prophet Muhammad ﷺ. The Prophet saw that there was some mark of perfume on his shirt. So the Prophet

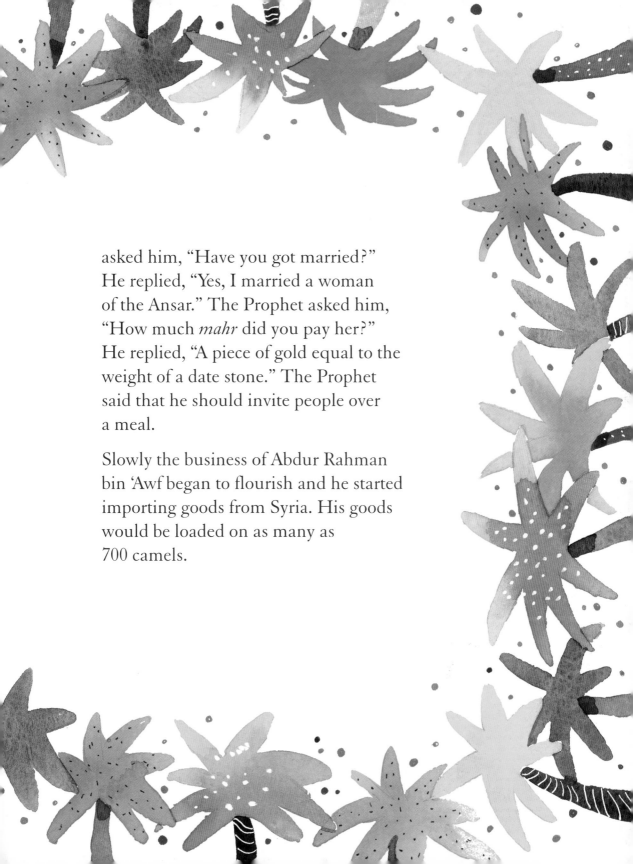

asked him, "Have you got married?" He replied, "Yes, I married a woman of the Ansar." The Prophet asked him, "How much *mahr* did you pay her?" He replied, "A piece of gold equal to the weight of a date stone." The Prophet said that he should invite people over a meal.

Slowly the business of Abdur Rahman bin 'Awf began to flourish and he started importing goods from Syria. His goods would be loaded on as many as 700 camels.

The Caravan of Abdur Rahman bin 'Awf

Once, after the death of the Prophet, the caravan of Abdur Rahman bin 'Awf comprising of 1000 camels carrying goods from Syria entered Madinah. There was so much merchandise that it took 1000 camels to carry it all. Naturally there was great chaos and a lot of noise. A big crowd of curious onlookers gathered to see the caravan. The air was very hazy with dust as the camels reached the centre as Madinah, as if a big dust storm had covered the entire city. At that time the Prophet's wife, 'Aishah was in her house. When she heard all this

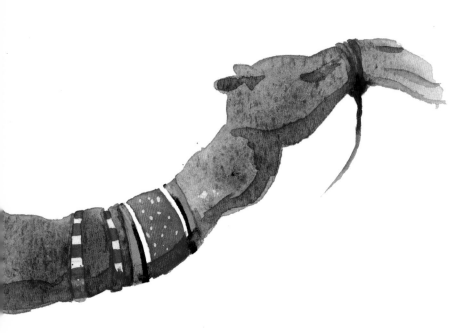

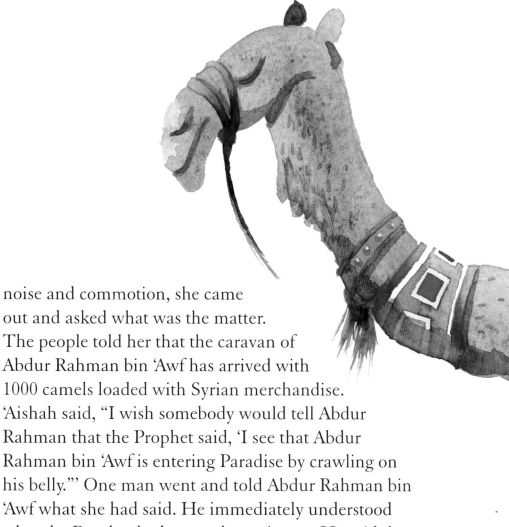

noise and commotion, she came out and asked what was the matter. The people told her that the caravan of Abdur Rahman bin 'Awf has arrived with 1000 camels loaded with Syrian merchandise. 'Aishah said, "I wish somebody would tell Abdur Rahman that the Prophet said, 'I see that Abdur Rahman bin 'Awf is entering Paradise by crawling on his belly.'" One man went and told Abdur Rahman bin 'Awf what she had said. He immediately understood what the Prophet had meant by saying so. He said that perhaps the Prophet meant that since he was so much involved in business that he was not able to do justice to the *dawah* mission, and had made worldly affairs his sole concern in life. But this was not true. Then he said, "I will try to enter Paradise on foot rather than crawling on my belly." He immediately donated all his merchandise, including the 1000 camels to the cause of Allah.

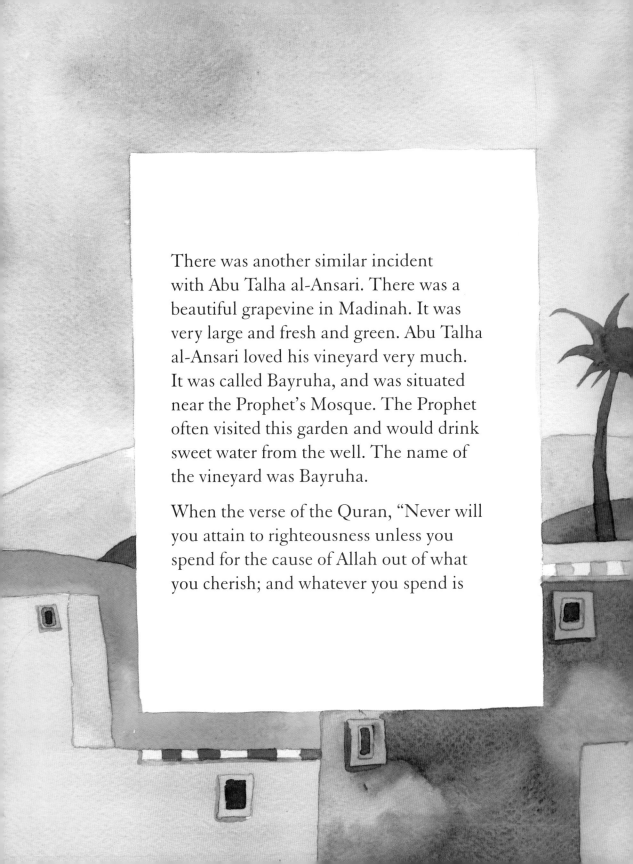

There was another similar incident with Abu Talha al-Ansari. There was a beautiful grapevine in Madinah. It was very large and fresh and green. Abu Talha al-Ansari loved his vineyard very much. It was called Bayruha, and was situated near the Prophet's Mosque. The Prophet often visited this garden and would drink sweet water from the well. The name of the vineyard was Bayruha.

When the verse of the Quran, "Never will you attain to righteousness unless you spend for the cause of Allah out of what you cherish; and whatever you spend is

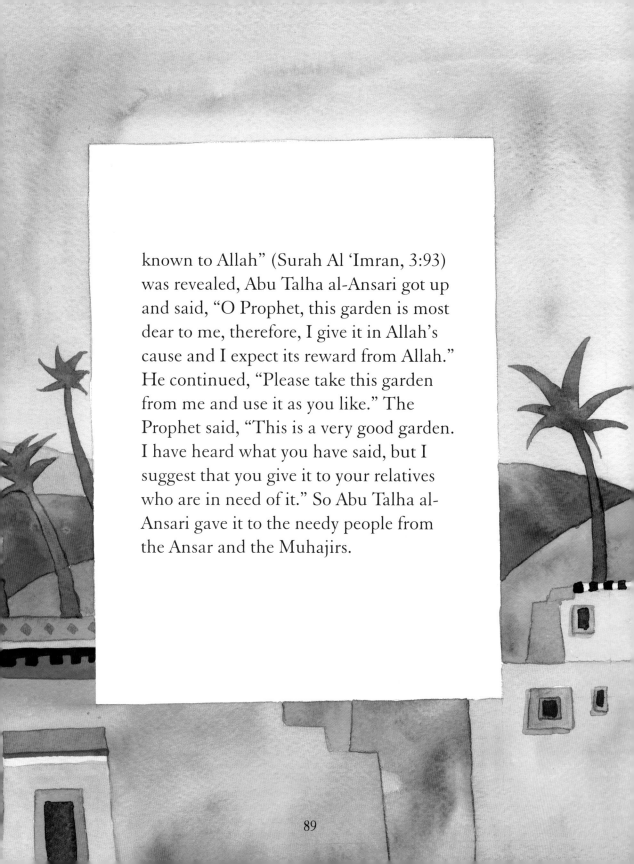

known to Allah" (Surah Al 'Imran, 3:93) was revealed, Abu Talha al-Ansari got up and said, "O Prophet, this garden is most dear to me, therefore, I give it in Allah's cause and I expect its reward from Allah." He continued, "Please take this garden from me and use it as you like." The Prophet said, "This is a very good garden. I have heard what you have said, but I suggest that you give it to your relatives who are in need of it." So Abu Talha al-Ansari gave it to the needy people from the Ansar and the Muhajirs.

The Ansar were mainly farmers. They owned date palm orchards. The Ansar said to the Prophet Muhammad ﷺ that he should divide their orchards equally among their brothers, the Muhajirs. The Muhajirs, however, did not know anything about farming, because they were mainly merchants. Therefore, the Prophet Muhammad ﷺ told them not to give them their fields and orchards. The Prophet said, "The Muhajirs will not be able to manage them, so you give them the value of half of the produce and keep half for yourselves." The Ansar happily agreed to this.

In this way, the relationship of the Muhajirs and the Ansar became a real one. It is mentioned in the Sahih al-Bukhari that when one of the Ansar died, the Muhajir Companion would get a share of his property.

The Change of Qiblah

When the Prophet Muhammad ﷺ was in Makkah, he and his Companions – the Sahabah – prayed towards the Kabah. The Kabah remained the *qiblah* or the prayer direction for 13 years. But when the Prophet and his Companions migrated from Makkah to Madinah, the Prophet made the Dome of the Rock in Jerusalem the *qiblah*.

The Prophet and his Companions prayed toward Jerusalem for 16 months. The Prophet did this to soften the hearts of the Jews who lived in Madinah. This was so that there should not be any unnecessary conflict between the Muslims and other religious groups of Madinah. It was better if they all remained in a peaceful atmosphere, so that the *dawah* work, or spreading the message of the Quran to all people, could be done without any hindrance. But the Jews, out of pride, would tell people that Muhammad had come to their religion.

After 16 months, Allah commanded the believers to now change their *qiblah*. Instead of praying towards the Dome of the Rock, or *Qubbat al-Sakhra*, they were to pray towards the Kabah in Makkah. Allah's command came as a revelation in the Quran.

It is set forth in the following verses:

"The foolish will ask, 'What has made them turn away from their direction of prayer which they used to face?' Say, 'The East and the West belong to God. He guides whom He pleases to the right path.' Thus We have made you a middle nation, so that you may act as witnesses for mankind, and the Messenger may be a witness for you." (Al-Baqarah, 2:142-143).

When the Prophet saw that the Jews due to their way of thinking were not responding to the Prophet's praying towards Jerusalem, but were taking it in a negative sense, the Prophet wanted to return to the original prayer direction, that is towards the Kabah in Makkah. Once when the Prophet was leading the Asr prayer in Madinah, the following verse was revealed.

"Wherever you come from, turn your face to the Sacred Mosque; wherever you may be, turn your faces towards it, so that people will not have any argument against you except for the wrongdoers among them. Do not fear them; fear Me, so that I may perfect My favour to you and you may be rightly guided." (2:150)

As the Prophet received the verse, right in the middle of the prayers, he, along with all the Companions who were praying with him, turned away from Jerusalem and faced in the direction of Makkah.

One of the Companions who was praying with the Prophet when the prayer direction was changed said that he passed by another mosque in Madinah. He saw that people were still praying towards Jerusalem. So he told the people there that that he had said his prayers with the Prophet towards the Kabah. Hearing this, all the people there too turned towards the Kabah. In this way all the Muslims started praying towards Makkah and stopped praying towards Jerusalem.

Seeing this the Jews of Madinah began to say, "See what kind of Prophet is this who changes his prayer direction every now and then."

The Quran emphasises that the acceptance of worship is based on the spirit, in which it is done, and not just on the form. In this way, the Muslims were taught what real virtue was. Then the following verses of the Quran were revealed:

"Virtue does not consist in whether you face towards the East or the West; virtue means believing in God, the Last Day, the angels, the Book and the prophets; the virtuous are those who, despite their love for it, give away their wealth to their relatives and to orphans and the very poor, and to travellers and those who ask [for charity], and to set slaves free, and who attend to their prayers and pay the alms, and who keep their pledges when they make them, and show patience in hardship and adversity, and in times of distress. Such are the true believers; and such are the God-fearing." (2:177)

Bibliography

A. Guillaume, *The Life of Muhammad: A Translation of Ibn Ishaq's Sirat Rasul Allah,* Oxford University Press, Karachi, 1967.

Ali Muhammad al-Sallabi, *Al-Sirah al-Nabawiyah*, Dar Ibn Kathir, Damascus, 2007.

Dr. Farida Khanam, *The Life of the Prophet Muhammad made simple*, Goodword Books, New Delhi, 2013

Ibn Hisham, *al-Sirah al-Nabawiyyah*, Dar al-Qalam, Beirut, 2009.

Ibn Kathir, *Al-Sirah al-Nabawiyyah*, Darul Fikr, Beirut, 1978.

Maulana Shibli Nu'mani, *Sirat-un-Nabi*, Kitab Bhavan, Delhi, 2008.

Maulana Wahiduddin Khan, *The Prophet Muhammad: A Simple Guide*, Goodword Books, New Delhi, 2007.

Maulana Wahiduddin Khan, *Sirat-e-Rasul,* Goodword Books, New Delhi, 2009.

Maulana Wahiduddin Khan, *The Prophet of Peace*, Penguin Books, New Delhi, 2009.

Maulana Wahiduddin Khan, *Muhammad: A Prophet for All Humanity*, Goodword Books, New Delhi, 2011.

Muhammad Husayn Haykal, *Life of Muhammad*, New Crescent Publishing Company, New Delhi, 2009.

Saniyasnain Khan, *Tell Me About the Prophet Muhammad*, Goodword Books, New Delhi, 2008.